"Emma"

Sanja Mach

Copyright © Sanja Mach
All rights reserved. This book or parts thereof may not be reproduced, photocopied, translated, stored in a database of distributed in any form or by any means (electronic, optical, or mechanical, including photocopying or recording), without the express written and signed consent of the author.

Self – publishing
Print on demand

Language reviewer Željana Pavlaković and Multikatedra d.o.o. Center for translations and education
Edited by Calvin Allen

ISBN 9798653627736

This book belongs to:

"" ""

Emma

Sanja Mach

Illustrator   Al'ona Mytrofanova

Split, 2020

On the way home, Emma passed between tall, gray buildings with many windows.

Although her house was located in another part of the town, she always preferred to walk rather than ride the bus like the other children.

She preferred to go this longer way because she would always meet someone she knew, whether from school or her street, and thus learn something new.

People like to chat when they meet on the road, and our Emma was a proper little chatterbox.

But on what was a seemingly ordinary day, she saw something different on her route.

On an old wooden bench sat a young girl about her age, no different to the others except that she wore a red bow in her hair that was larger than her head. Emma was amazed to see that this made her head look really tiny, like the tip of a pin!

Emma, who was very curious, was attracted by this interesting-looking girl, and so she approached her and asked politely, "Excuse me, may I join you?"

The girl looked at her, gave her a broad smile and answered cheerfully: "Of course! Sit down!" The girl moved up to make space for Emma.

"Thanks!" Emma said graciously and then continued, "Are you waiting for someone?"

"Maybe," the little girl answered enigmatically.

"And what's your name?" Emma continued her questions.

"Hope," answered the girl, very briefly.

"My name is Emma and I'm very happy to meet you!"

Hope sat silently, smiling to herself but continuing to gaze at the big gray building in front of her without looking at Emma at all.

Emma thought that this was rather rude of her but, after a brief hesitation, decided to ask another question.

"You know, uh ..." she paused a little before continuing, "Your bow is very, very large. May I ask you why it's so big?"

The girl continued to stare in front of her without answering Emma's question.

This made Emma very impatient, but she decided not to rush Hope for an answer and wait a while longer. But she also resolved that, if Hope didn't answer her soon, she would politely say goodbye and go home because the only reason Emma had stopped was to find out why this unusual girl had such a big bow in her hair.

Just when Emma was about to leave, Hope began to speak.
"This bow, that made you so curious, is the device that will take me back to the future."

Not in her wildest dreams did Emma expect such an answer. "You mean something like a time machine?" She bustled with excitement at Hope's sentence.

"Yes, precisely that, a kind of time machine!"

Emma sat there utterly shocked with her mouth open and her eyes as large as two round saucers.

"But that's not possible," she said, more to herself. "Alright, so you are from the future."

"Yes!" Hope replied cheerily while still
gazing across the street at this completely ordinary,
tall, gray building with many windows,
the same as all the others in the street.

"And how does this device work?"
Emma pursued the question, ignoring that Hope
was not looking at her while talking;
oh no, she was still staring at the building
opposite, quite obsessively.

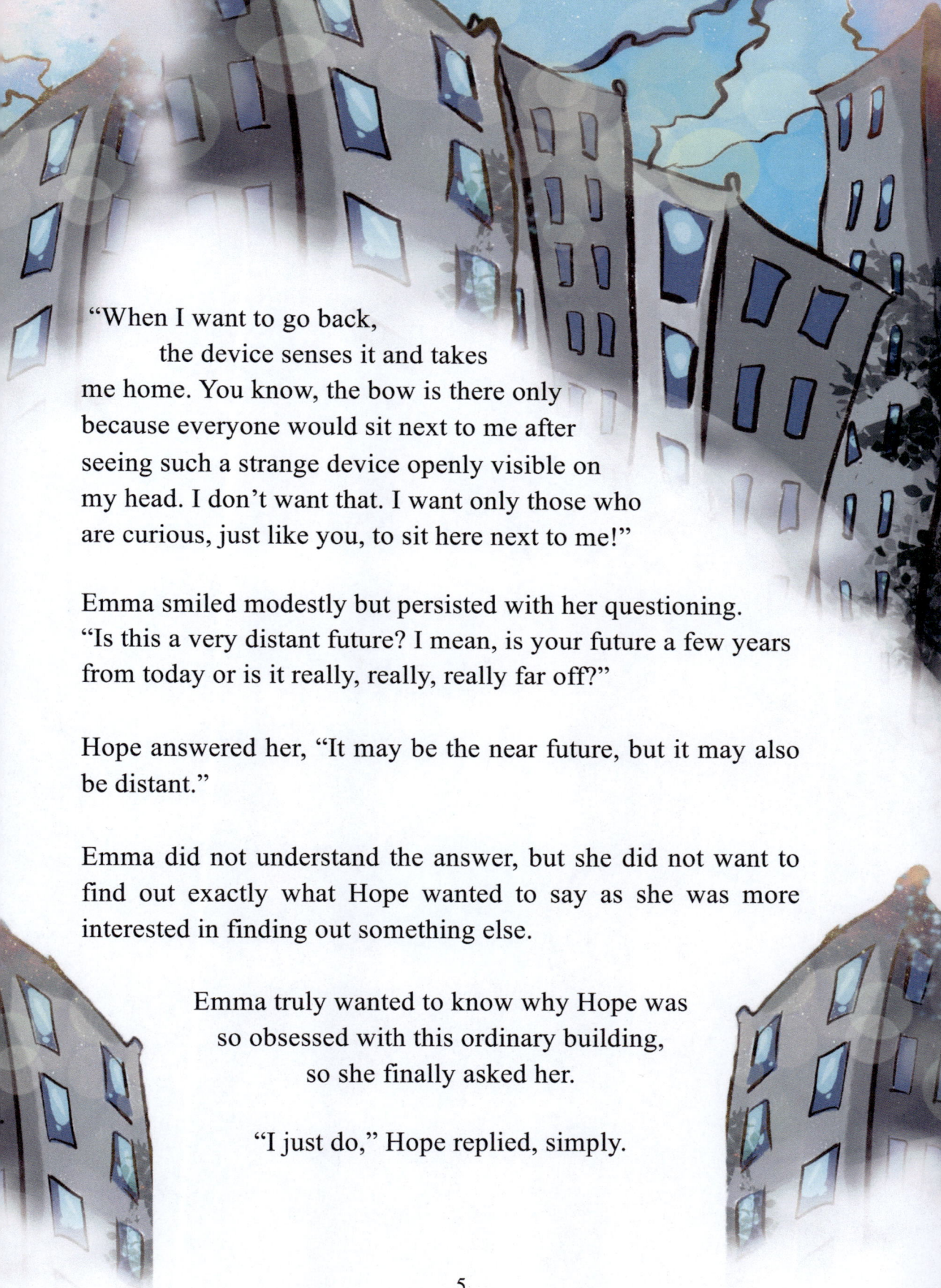

"When I want to go back, the device senses it and takes me home. You know, the bow is there only because everyone would sit next to me after seeing such a strange device openly visible on my head. I don't want that. I want only those who are curious, just like you, to sit here next to me!"

Emma smiled modestly but persisted with her questioning. "Is this a very distant future? I mean, is your future a few years from today or is it really, really, really far off?"

Hope answered her, "It may be the near future, but it may also be distant."

Emma did not understand the answer, but she did not want to find out exactly what Hope wanted to say as she was more interested in finding out something else.

Emma truly wanted to know why Hope was so obsessed with this ordinary building, so she finally asked her.

"I just do," Hope replied, simply.

"Well, if you are from the future, what would I see here in your time?" asked Emma, again offended by such rudeness.

"Nothing!" answered Hope even more abruptly than before.

Emma was already quite cross because, when she tells a story, she explains everything down to the finest detail and getting any extra word out of this Hope was like pulling teeth.

"Uh…" sighed Emma, unaware that her thoughts were changing her mood.

Hope seemed to feel Emma's restlessness, so she explained, "Do you see this building there and this street running between us and it?" Emma nodded.

"In the future, there's a big meadow there with wild, galloping horses. It is a beautiful sight to see, as you can imagine. It takes your breath away to watch them running freely like that, with the wind blowing their manes all over the place!"

"Really?" Emma was surprised again. She has never seen a wild horse before, or any other wild creature whatsoever, except on television, and she thought how lovely it would be to see them like that.

"Yes, and what remains of this building is only a memory of how people lost their lives to concrete, becoming isolated and disconnected from the natural world."

"But wait …………… where do you live now?" Emma asked curiously.

"We live like you do in homes, but in harmony with nature and connected to one another. In the place where I come from, everyone is friends with each other, and we help one another."

"That sounds lovely too," Emma thought, and then an idea came to her, suddenly, like her bedside light which she would turn on against her fear of the dark: "But if it's so lovely there, why are you here?"

Hope looked at her with a smile: "I'm here to warn children like you to do everything in their power to make such a future happen because, otherwise, the world won't have that future. You know, it is a very delicate thing, and there will always be people who do not want the sort of future I come from."

Hope paused for a second before proceeding in a serious tone:
"Emma, people make a terrible mistake by thinking that the future is just theirs alone: the future cannot be owned. It belongs to everyone equally."

"But does that mean there are more kids like you?" Emma asked.

"Yes! And there are children like you. Right at this moment, another girl is sitting on another bench in another town, telling a curious girl or boy the same story if he or she cares to hear it."

"Alright, what should I do?"

Hope answered her like this: "You have to tell everyone you know what I told you; and also everyone you don't know because you can only achieve this goal if you work together."

Then, suddenly, she just disappeared, as if she had never been there at all.

Emma shivered, but now she knew that everything Hope had told her was true.

Up until that moment, she had doubted the truth of Hope's story, but now she was no longer in doubt; now she knew what her job was.

She rushed home and immediately sat down at her desk.

She took a big block of paper and pens of all colors.

She loved bright colors the most; those were the right ones.

She could emphasize what was important with them because not everything was as significant as this.

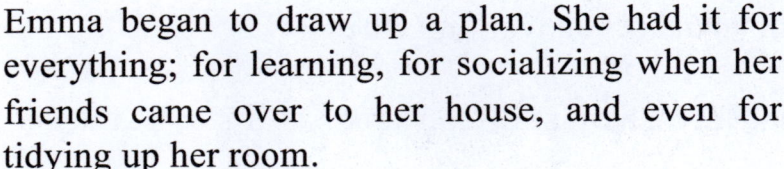

Emma began to draw up a plan. She had it for everything; for learning, for socializing when her friends came over to her house, and even for tidying up her room.

But now, she needed to develop an essential strategy and try her hardest to make it her best plan ever.

First, she decided to find everyone who had met little girls with big bows in their hair and find out if they had their own plans; and then change the world with them.

Then, she decided to do this by teaching people how to love each other, to protect nature, and to believe that they can do anything if they do it together.

Years went by, and the voice of Emma and her friends spread across the world.

Emma grew up into a fine woman
and, over the years, her persistence
in realizing the plan she came up with
when she was ten years old
did not diminish.

And so, one sunny day,
as she walked to her house,
down the same street she had walked so many
times before, she noted that she was
continually walking in the shade.
But it was not the shade of tall, gray buildings
but from a canopy of large trees that
people had planted along the road.

A smile appeared on her face; and then
she noticed the same little girl sitting
on the same wooden bench.

Emma approached her and asked her politely, "May I sit down?"

Hope turned to her: "Of course Emma, I have been waiting for you!"

Emma looked at her with surprise: "I beg your pardon?"

Hope seemed as though she did not notice the look on Emma's face: "I knew you would change the world and make it beautiful. That is why I came today to tell you that you have succeeded!"

And, as she said that, she disappeared into thin air like she did the first time so many years ago.

Emma lingered for a while, sitting on the bench, calm and contented as all her hard work had paid off.

Not only does the world have a future, but it has a beautiful one at that, with wild horses and meadows full of flowers.

Emma was so proud because she and her friends had made it happen.

About The Author

Sanja Mach was born in Split, Croatia on June 6, 1980. She graduated from the University of Split, Croatia with a degree in Economics.
Sanja is mother to Frane (11) and Anja (8) who are the very reason she discovered creative writing
and her love of storytelling.

She writes fiction and stories for children.
This is her third story published on Amazon. Besides this book for children, she has written "Curious Gecko" and "The Crowd in the Ocean".

Printed in Great Britain
by Amazon